Welcome To Truly Into Poetry

Welcome to the world of T.I.P.

Truly into Poetry is where you need to be

The door is always open, you can come on in

To entertain the world with thoughts from my pen

Come check out some of the words that I like

You can check it out either day or night

You can also find me on Twitter, Tumblr and Facebook

Once you get into my poetry you will be hook

So leave me a message and tell me what you think

A successful poetry book is on the brink

Copyright 2010 by Tiffany Taylor. All Rights Reserved.

No part of this book shall be or reproduce, distributed, or transmitted by any form or any means, or stores in a database or retrieval system, without the prior permission of the author.

Printed in the United States of America

First Edition August 2010

ISBN # 978-0-615-39633-0

Editor: Tina Tatum
Forward by LaKina Johnson

Contact Info:
Email: wheatieb@yahoo.com
Twitter: www.twitter.com/Trulyintopoetry
Facebook: www.facebook.com
www.trulyintopoetry.com

Preface

Truly Into Poetry was written because I wanted to do something different. I wanted to show people that you can do anything when you put your mind to it, no matter what your background is I have been writing poetry since the third grade but never thought about writing a book. My parents read all of the material that I wrote, so in high school my parents gave me the idea to turn my work into a book. But, it never happened, because I didn't know how to go about it and I did not think that my material was good enough to put into a book. So I kept writing and other people would read my material and ask why I hadn't considered writing a book. So I decided to do research on how to get started on writing a poetry book, and it was easier than I thought. The more research I did, the more I realize how big this field was. I was meeting people who were giving me advice and helping me through the process. I even considered having some of my material turned into music.

Truly Into Poetry is just a collection of poetry that I have written over the years. Some of the poems are personal and some are not but most of the poems in this book are written to leave the reader with something to think about. But others are fun and are just meant to be laughed at.

Dedication

I would like to thank God and my parents; Ann Taylor and Reno Lilly for giving me the talent to write and also for supporting me in this journey. My little sister; Erika Taylor for telling if my work was good or bad

Acknowledgements

First I would like to thank Kolayah KeeVan for helping me through this journey and supporting me in time of need. Also, I would like to thank Shani Greene-Dowdell for keeping me on the right path at times of confusion, Tina Tatum for editing Truly Into Poetry, and last, but not least, LaKina Johnson for helping me with ideas when I had writer's block and for writing my forward.

Thank you guys! I could not have done this without you.

About the Author

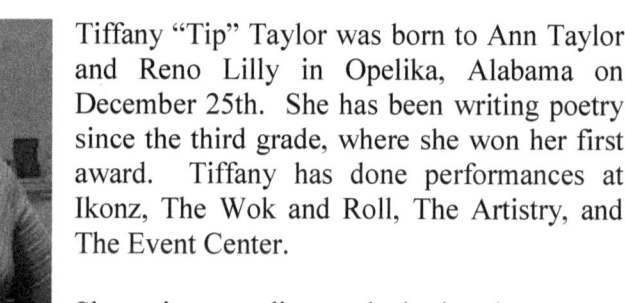

Tiffany "Tip" Taylor was born to Ann Taylor and Reno Lilly in Opelika, Alabama on December 25th. She has been writing poetry since the third grade, where she won her first award. Tiffany has done performances at Ikonz, The Wok and Roll, The Artistry, and The Event Center.

She enjoys reading and sharing her poetry with others. Tiffany eventually would like to have some of her poetry turned into music and hopefully one day to become a ghost writer.

Tiffany also enjoys music, movies and working on computers. She is a graduate of Auburn University with a degree in Political Science.

Forward

Tiffany is a true poet and author who wrote this book out of love. It is very hard for someone to give you all of them, but in this book she has. Now, you must read this. As a person who knows what a good book is, this is food for the soul. This is written to truly inspire inspiration, to give order to chaos. Her hopes and dreams are only for those who read her poetic words can relate. I feel reading her words is like going to church. When the preacher speaks and you feel like he is talking to you. Her dedication has led to this book…a compilation of poetic works that she would love to share. I may be a fan, but I too love good literary work.

Today is the day that you are blessed to relieve and receive a spiritual awakening. My hopes are that you will feel as passionate about this work as I do. Everybody has a gift and Tiffany's true weapon is her pen. She has created a super masterpiece and I am happy with her letting me take part to make readers happy. I would like to introduce Tiffany Taylor aka TIP.

Never stop entertaining the world with thoughts from your pen.

Lakina Johnson

Table of Content

Mistake --- 1
Missing You --- 3
Ode to a Sorry Ass Man --- 4
Screams in the Night --- 6
Stalkers --- 7
The Cycle --- 9
The Pain --- 11
What I Want --- 12
Backstabber --- 13
Bad Off --- 16
Black People --- 18
Bullshit --- 20
Hungry --- 23
Apart --- 24
First Breakup --- 25
Cheater I --- 26
Cheater II --- 27
Bite My Ass --- 28
14 Lines for Valentine --- 29
Crazy --- 30
Crystal Clear --- 31
Drop Back In --- 32
Go Away --- 33
Graduation --- 34
Him --- 35
I Am --- 37
I Am Woman --- 38
I'm Different --- 40
I Give Up --- 41
I Love You Because --- 42
Immaturity --- 44
Jaws --- 45
Intoxicated --- 46
Labor Day --- 47
Leaving --- 48
Lonely Hallways --- 49

Love Hurts	50
Soul Mate	51
Can't Figure Out	53
Distraught	54
It Doesn't Require Me To Have Balls	56
Patiently Waiting	58
Strangers in the Street	61
The Bottle	63
The House on the Block	66
Abandonment	68
Bills	71
Christmas Has Ended at 29	73
The Way	75
Be Happy With What You Got	76
Good Enough to be Your Girl but Not Your Wife	77
Lies	79
Love	81
Why Worry	84
Time Brings Along change	86

Truly Into Poetry by Tiffany Taylor

Mistake

The news I'm about to tell you, you won't believe
What you are about to hear, won't put your mind at ease
I did something wrong, I hate to admit
But it's going to make our marriage more complicated
First of all let me tell you, how much I love you
And you know that I'll do anything for you
But there comes a time when there are changes in your life
And dealing with the sacrifices of being a wife
I thought about this long and hard, about what I'm going to say
And I know you are going to hate me in every way
You remember two years ago, when you were overseas
When I did this I wasn't thinking about the risk and possibilities
I was feeling so depressed and all alone
Wishing that you were coming home
I tried my best to keep my mind occupied
I was so emotional and sometimes even cried
Someone came over to keep me company, while you were gone
And to ease some of the discomfort of being alone
But I guess he came over, one time too many
Something came over, something was in me
I slept with someone in our bed
The very same place where you lay your head
I am so sorry that I did this to you
But you've got more bad news that's about to come through

Truly Into Poetry by Tiffany Taylor

What you are about to hear is a whole lot worse
You're gonna say "Oh my God, "have I been cursed"
What happened, has happened, the damage has been done
But the baby you have been taking care of is not your son
I cried like a baby, when I finally found out
Feeling tired, pain and all stressed out
I have already made this confession to your mother
But the baby that you love belongs to your brother
My heart hurts for you because I know I did you wrong
Because I kept this secret from you for so long
By the tears in your eyes and the expression on your face
That part of my life I wish I could erase
But I do understand and I'll do what it takes
But I can't even forgive myself, because this is my mistake.

Truly Into Poetry by Tiffany Taylor

Missing You

Is there anything to take the pain away?
Is there anything anybody can say?
The way I am feeling when you are gone
All I do is sit around and moan
I never knew it would feel this bad
Feel so low, Feel so sad
When you're not here, it feels like part of me is gone
Although I have everything, I still feel alone
Is this some type of torture, life is putting me through
Going through the day wondering when will I see you
I miss your face, I miss your voice, and I miss your smile
Every day seems as long as a mile
I look at your picture and see your smiling face
And sometimes wish that time would race away
Going to your house without getting upset is not easy to do
Because I know I'm not there with you
Getting your phone calls makes me feel better and glad
Even though I'm still feeling sad
I have a feeling that this pain is not going to go away
So I guess I'll get used to not seeing you every day

Truly Into Poetry by Tiffany Taylor

Ode to a Sorry Ass Man

There is one thing in life that I can't stand
It's when I come across a sorry ass man
He doesn't have shit
He can't stand on his own
He always depends on somebody, even though he's grown
He wants to have sex but not the responsibility of kids
He doesn't want to be responsible for anything that he did
Most of the time he lives at home with mom
Or lives with a woman who is really, really dumb
He drives her car and stays away for hours
When I look at him all I see is a coward
He wants to have money but can't keep a job
Every time you're around him it feels like you're being robbed
He has no ambition or goals
Just being with him can take your very soul
He wants to live the carefree life without rules and regulations
He is always making someone's life more complicated
I don't know where he came from but I wish he would go back
Stressing everybody out like a heart attack
He also has a habit of putting his hands on somebody
Always thinks he can hit somebody

If you know someone like this, I hope he is not your man
You're better off being a single woman

Truly Into Poetry by Tiffany Taylor

If this describes you, your ass should be ashamed
Get your shit together and stop being lame
People are tired of taking care of yo' stank ass
It's really becoming an un-useful task
The only thing you are doing is taking up space
You are nothing but a bunch of waste
I wish there was a law to get rid of you as fast as I can
Cause I'm tired of being around *a sorry ass man*

I hope you enjoyed the official…

Ode to a Sorry Ass Man

Truly Into Poetry by Tiffany Taylor

Screams In The Night

Hear the sound of glass shattering
...as a scream breaks through the light
Hear the sound of the headless horseman
... galloping through the night
Hear the sound of crunching bones as someone takes a bite
Hear the sound of windows and doors being locked up tight
Hear the sound of rustling like a torn shattered kite
Hear the sound of screams and the woman's face turns white
Hear the sound of a ghost disappearing out of sight
Hear the sound of a car running off the cliff at the right
Hear the sound of terror as someone falls from a distant height
Hear the stories of the tale of fright night

Truly Into Poetry by Tiffany Taylor

Stalker

The first time I saw you, you were with your boys
Just looking at you brought me lots of joy
The second time I saw you, you were with your wife
But I didn't care I wanted to be in your life
I knew where you worked, ate and played
I took time out to see you every day
The way you are walking, the way you are talking
Damn I can't believe this, you've got me stalking
I can't believe I did this but I broke in your house
While you were in the bed sleeping with your spouse
But all I wanted was a piece of clothing that I could hold
And a picture that I could hang on the wall like a centerfold
I see you playing with your kids in the park
Your body is so flawless it's like a work of art
You're a breath of fresh air; I've got to breathe you in
But the way I feel about you has got to be a sin
I moved across the street to be close to you
Looking out the kitchen window playing peek -a -boo
On the days you leave for work, I make sure that I am up
So I can see you get ready and get in your truck
During my lunch break, I come to your job to see you work
I know your daily schedule like clockwork

Truly Into Poetry by Tiffany Taylor

I told my sister that I was in love with this man
That I was trying my best to be his #1 fan
When I first saw you that's when the stalking began
But after a year will this come to an end

(To be continued)

Truly Into Poetry by Tiffany Taylor

The Cycle

Newborn babies coming into the world
It could be a boy or a girl
Some babies have hair and some are bald
But parents just want them healthy, that's all

When you get them home they cry all night
And hold their little fists tight
When they are little they don't get into too much trouble
All they do is lie around and blow bubbles

But the toddler stage is where the trouble begins
It's the worst stage that they are in
They run around with nothing but their diapers on
And half of them think they are about grown

They tear up things and get into stuff
The parents just about have enough
Now it's time for kindergarten, first, second grade
And the parents thinking they've got it made

Then comes third, fourth, and fifth
Now they want big humongous gifts
Here comes sixth, seventh, and eighth

Truly Into Poetry by Tiffany Taylor

Now parents are feeling great
Oh! Now here comes high school
That's when everyone starts acting a fool
Driving fast in their brand new car
When the police get behind them they won't get very far

Boys look at girls and girls look at boys
They're buying each other gifts and little stuffed toys
Here comes graduation, the greatest day of all
Now you're ready to do to a party and have a ball

Now you have a job and work the whole summer
Oh! No back to school, what a bummer
You're head for college, to get a career
Now you know the time to leave home is near

You out of college it's time to get married
Here comes you and your husband with the baby carriage
Now you wish yourself good luck on a four leaf clover
Because the cycle for you has just started over

Truly Into Poetry by Tiffany Taylor

The Pain

The pain you feel after a breakup
You will be all messed up
And you don't know what's up

The pain you feel is like no other
Because it comes from another
The feeling makes you shudder

It's hard to get rid of the pain
So being by yourself you will contain
Because you want to save the unbroken part of your heart that remains

Truly Into Poetry by Tiffany Taylor

What I Want

What I want is a strong powerful man
Doing all that he possibly can
I want someone to brush my teeth with at night
When I'm upset, someone to hold me tight
Someone to hold my hand for no reason at all
Just to say hello with a phone call
Someone to feed me chicken soup when I am sick
Someone who knows me and what makes me tick
I want someone to kiss me just because I am there
Someone who loves me without a care
Someone to give me back massages and rub my feet
Someone who is not always so neat
I want someone who gives me respect
Someone who is not always perfect
Someone who is there without me asking them to
Someone who will support me in whatever I do
I want a relationship that is strong
And hope that nothing goes wrong
I want someone I can do stuff with
Someone I can watch television with
I want someone who is like no other
Doesn't even have to be a brother
I want someone who is true
I want someone just like you

Truly Into Poetry by Tiffany Taylor

Backstabber

What happens when your friends do you wrong
And you have no place where you belong
You can never tell who your real friends are
They can really cut you so deep and leave a scar

No one to talk to, no one to call your friend
And that's just how my story begins
I had this best friend; we were friends for a long time
What she did to me really caught me by surprise

We used to hang out all the time and have lots of fun
All day in the streets we would run
You were like my sister, you were like my fam
What you did to me, I knew you didn't give a damn

But I even trusted you with my life
When you did this, you were not thinking twice
You knew Marcus and I had been dating for some time
You knew we would do anything for each other
...at the drop of a dime

We even lived together and talked about making it official
But I realize that those dreams were only superficial
But you were the one who put us together

Truly Into Poetry by Tiffany Taylor

But I never thought you would become the regretter

If you wanted him for yourself, why did you set us up?
But you trying to get him back, now that's really fucked up
You knew I would be out -of -town on a business trip
Because you knew if I found out, my ass would flip

But I knew the two of you were together for a fact
Because both of you were acting real funny when I got back
I knew y'all were planning something all along
I had butterflies in my stomach, I knew something was wrong

You used to come by my house all of the time
But now it seems like you never have the time
But I made it seem like I didn't know a thing
That I was all ready to wear Marcus's ring

But since the two of you want to be together
I will make it permanent, so y'all can be together forever
So I told the two of you I had to go out of town
Hoping y'all would meet for a second round

So I waited around for you to get to my home
The two of you wanted to make sure that y'all were all alone
While y'all were at it I snuck into the house
Tip Toeing being quiet as a mouse

Truly Into Poetry by Tiffany Taylor

I heard y'all moaning and groaning upstairs
Y'all were going at it without a care
I decided to wait until the two of you were sleeping
I guess y'all were tired from all that creeping

So I came back upstairs with a can of gas
Y'all had no idea I was about to rotisserie, yawl's ass
I poured gas all over the two of you and the bed
If y'all had known the deal, you would have fled

I woke the two of you before I struck the match
So y'all could see what y'all were about to catch
There was nothing y'all could do, nothing to be said
I only heard y'all scream as I tossed the match on the bed

Truly Into Poetry by Tiffany Taylor

Bad Off

I'm on welfare and I can't pay my rent
I'm as broke as hell and I don't have a cent
I owe money to the mob and everyone else
Maybe I'll go ahead and shoot myself
I live in a two bedroom apartment with five bad ass kids
The apartment is full of cockroaches and a rat named Sid
My children have no shoes and no food to eat
Their shirts have holes and their pants no seats
My bills are past due, my children have nappy heads
My apartment is nasty and I have cooties in my bed
I can't find a job because of my education
I can't do anything to better my situation
My man is no good and he can't keep a job
All he wants to do is look at TV and eat like a slob
He doesn't help me out or give me any money
But he always has some, now isn't that funny
I get no help from my family, even though they could help me out
My nerves have gotten so bad I want to scream and shout
I walk around all day wondering what to do next
The only things I have in my life are regrets
I also worry about where my children's next meal is coming from
If I could feed them, the only thing I would eat would be gum
I tried to get food stamps but they weren't nearly enough
Why does society have to make it so tough?
I am on my own with no help in sight

Truly Into Poetry by Tiffany Taylor

I'm trying to fight this pain with all my might
I guess I should have made better decisions when I was young
When I was in school and my life had just begun
My life as I got older would have been better off
But I am in too deep and I will forever be bad off

Truly Into Poetry by Tiffany Taylor

Black People

Black People what's wrong with us today
We've always got something negative to say
We're always blaming someone else for our problems
Instead of taking the time out to solve them
And for once in our life can we be on time
Besides getting in the club free before nine

There's no reason for us not to get an education
After all the time we spent being segregated
We have so many opportunities for the good life
But instead we waste our time just rolling dice
We're always getting ourselves in stupid situations
And always try to make life more complicated

Black people, let's stop trying to get on the grind
And get an education before we get left behind
Can we please stop hating when someone gets ahead
Just because they work hard and have a little bread
And black people, can we stop fooling our kids
Making them think they have to rap to make it big

Let them know there is something more than spinning rims
And wearing the baggy jeans with the tims

Truly Into Poetry by Tiffany Taylor

We just made history in 2008
That all blacks one day can make it great
Don't think that you can't do the impossible
You can overcome any obstacle

When we all come together and function as one
With a little hard work, we can get the job done
It's been a long time coming; you can see what it was worth
But God says, who is last will one day be first.

Truly Into Poetry by Tiffany Taylor

Bullshit

The love I felt for you was like no other
I even took you home to meet my mother
Everything was all gravy for about six months
I didn't even realize that you were putting up a front

I dedicated my life to you, you were supposed to be my soul mate
But it was only my soul that you were trying to take
I meet you at a bar; you were hanging with your girls
I so much wanted to get into your world

I introduced myself just as a gentleman should
If I could take that day back, I wish I could
We went out a few times and I met your children
Never knew I could feel that close to them

You even spent the night at my house and we got our freak on
The next morning I told you that you didn't have to go home
Like I said before the 6 months was all gravy
I got to the point where I wanted you to have my baby

So I finally got the nerve to ask for your hand in marriage
I was the proud father with the baby carriage
But a month into the marriage, you begin acting strange
My entire life you begin to rearrange

Truly Into Poetry by Tiffany Taylor

You didn't like my friends anymore and didn't want them around the house
You said I didn't need them anymore; you were my friend and spouse
I was trying to understand where you were coming from
But you drew the line when you said I couldn't talk to my mom

You put rumors in the street that the baby was not mine
When I asked for a DNA test, you would decline
We would fuss and fight for no reason at all
You threw things at me and put holes in the wall

I saw a purchase on my credit card from a men's clothing store
But I knew it wasn't me that you made the purchase for
I confronted you about the purchase that you did
You said you wouldn't leave me because I have your kid

You busted the windows out of my car
When you thought I was talking to another woman
You didn't even apologize
When you found out it was my brother's girlfriend
You hang out all night, like I don't even exist
But there was something about you that I couldn't resist

I thought that I needed your love to help me grow
But now your ass needs to go

Truly Into Poetry by Tiffany Taylor

But there is some point in a man's life
That he needs to stop trying to turn a hoe into a wife

Like Usher said, "I'm ready to sign them papers"
And get rid of this entire caper
With you my life was a living hell
Just for being you I hope they put you in jail

No man should be with you, not even your daddy
Because you're nothing but a bitch and it comes out naturally
You give good women a bad name
Make a good woman hold her head in shame

After being married to you, I must call it quits
Because I am sick and tired of your Bullshit

Truly Into Poetry by Tiffany Taylor

Hungry

Pork chops, Ham Hock, Barbeque Ribs
So messy you need a bib
Collard Greens, Fatback, Cornbread cooked like no other
So good it makes you want to slap your grandmother
Fried Chicken with Macaroni and Cheese
Eat as much as you please
Corn on the Cob smothered in butter
So good it will make you stutter
Fish Sandwich and Coleslaw
No one cooks it like your grand maw
Baked Potato with Chives and Sour Cream
When it hits your mouth it will drop you to your knees
Apple Pie, Peach Cobbler and Ham Bone
It's so nice it will make you moan
Pizza, Steak and Sweet Potato Pie
You'll eat so much it will make you cry
Lasagna with Cheese and Bread with butter
No one cooks it better than your mother
Creamy Mashed Potatoes with gravy and Black Eyed Peas
Will make you give away your car keys
Fried Okra and Blackberry Pie
So good you'd thought you went to heaven and died

Truly Into Poetry by Tiffany Taylor

Apart

I miss you and you know it's true
Every day we're apart there's a hole in my heart
When you are gone, part of me is missing
And I wish you were at home
Being so far apart, it's kind of hard to reach you
And when I need you I can't pick up the phone
I feel you, I smell you, I see you in my dreams
I see you as my king and me as your queen
I feel lonely and sad inside
Although when I cry, I want to hide
There is a lonely feeling I want to hide
There is a lonely feeling I want to lose
Sometimes I feel bruised

I don't feel as bad as when you first left
I keep a positive outlook for myself
Some people say long distance relationships never work out
Although people who say that never have a relationship to talk about
Some people want to destroy what you have
Giving negative advice and backstab
Although we are far apart
It doesn't mean we don't have love in our hearts

Truly Into Poetry by Tiffany Taylor

First Breakup

I will never forget the day when we broke up
For the whole week I was all shaken up
I never have felt that bad in my whole life
Felt like I had been stabbed in the back with a knife

Like Tony Rich said, "Nobody Knows"
How my love for him grows and grows
I don't know why I still love him
But I wouldn't dare tell him

I can't go a day without mentioning his name
I guess I'm the only one to blame
Will I still love him after 10 years?
And go one without shedding a tear

I don't think I want another boyfriend
Every day I miss him
With all my heart
Now I wish we were never apart

Truly Into Poetry by Tiffany Taylor

Cheater 1

I can't understand why you left like you did
Cursed me out and rolled your eye lid
Why are you mad at me, I didn't cheat on you
That was some stupid shit you wanted to do
You're sleeping with someone else; I'm not keeping you in my house
So pack your rags and get the hell out
You're mad at me like I've done something wrong
Staying out with women all night long
Hey, I don't have to put up with this mess
You're giving me grey hair and causing me stress
You act like I'm the one who's a cheat
Coming home every night with your head looking like buck wheat
I don't have the patience and I don't have the time
I'm too young to be dealing with this in my prime
So don't call me, beep me or contact me in any kind of way
Just be with your other women and stay the hell away.

Truly Into Poetry by Tiffany Taylor

Cheater 2

You phone me and beep me constantly
Trying to get back with me
I told you over and over, I didn't want you back
Your crawling, begging and talking your smack
You should have thought about it before you cheated
Because you knew I was the one you needed
The woman you're with doesn't treat you right
She is coming in the house all time of night
But still your trying to make her your spouse
And you can't keep her in the house
When you do something wrong she jumps downs your throat
She always uses an excuse as a scapegoat
Sometimes when you sleep even though it's pretend
She slips out of the bed to the house of your best friend
I can see that you're losing your hair
That comes from a lot of wear and tear
You lost the best girl you ever had
Because she is driving you mad
What goes around, comes around
And you can learn from mistakes
But make too many mistakes and you'll have nothing but heartache

Truly Into Poetry by Tiffany Taylor

Bite My Ass

If I tell you to bite my ass that means leave me alone
If I tell you to bite my ass that means get the hell on
If I tell you to bite my ass that means shut the hell up
If I tell you to bite my ass that means I don't give a fuck
If I tell you to bite my ass that means you're wasting my time
If I tell you to bite my ass that means don't ask me for a dime
If I tell you to bite my ass that means move out of my damn way
If I tell you to bite my ass that means I don't have time to play
If I tell you to bite my ass that means you're getting on my nerves
If you don't like me I don't care because you can bite my ass

Truly Into Poetry by Tiffany Taylor

14 Lines for Valentines

The day you walked into my life, my whole world changed
From that day on I would never be the same
You got me wide open and feeling good
To always be with you, I wish I could
The way I feel when you're around
Like I'm on cloud 10 and there's no one that can bring me down
You give me support and a whole lot more
I'm always surprised and I never know what's in store
I wish I could fold you up and put you in my pocket
Or put you on a gold chain and wear you like a locket
You like me for who I am and you keep it real
I know I can do anything, that's how you make me feel
I feel so alone when we are apart
This poem I wrote for you is straight from the heart

Truly Into Poetry by Tiffany Taylor

Crazy

I watched you the other day and shook my head
And said to myself this girl must be crazy
Is there something in the universe
That makes you act like that
I tried to help you leave him but you refuse to leave
You played me for a fool and told me to leave you alone
But I'm not the one messing with you, it's him
Spending all the money when the rent is due
So you had to take the grocery money to pay the rent
He doesn't give you money to help with the bills
All he does is drink his money up
He sits on your couch, watches your TV and eats your food
And you don't say a word
I watched you the other day and shook my head
And said to myself this girl must be crazy

Truly Into Poetry by Tiffany Taylor

Crystal Clear

See Crystal Clear dribbling down the court
Everybody knows that b-ball is her ultimate sport
Don't get in her way; she'll shake you out of your shoes
When the ball's in her hand, you have nothing to lose
Dribble, Dribble, Bounce, Bounce
She will certainly fake you out
Watch her gracefulness, watch her moves
You from the court she will remove
Don't step out on the court unless you've got game
I learned from experience 'cause she put me to shame
Play Crystal Clear and you'll soon regret
When the ball goes in, it's nothing but net
Look out WNBA cause Crystal Clear is coming to play
With 7 rebounds and 20 points a game
The city of Auburn is from whence she came
So come and see Crystal play
I guaranteed she'll make your day

Truly Into Poetry by Tiffany Taylor

Drop Back In

Hey, Honey let me tell you from the start
Getting back in school would be very smart
The very first thing you need is an education
If you're ever going to make it in this nation
Being a black man with an education is hard enough
But being one without an education is even tougher
School is hard for all of us
Getting up early to catch the school bus
Nobody likes school, not even me
Having to stay there til after 3
But you try your best and keep a strong mind
Even though you may sometimes fall behind
Some of your friends are going to say, "Man do what you want to do".
But stay in school and one day, they'll be working for you
I know you are smart and you can do it
If you just put your mind to it
So think about getting back in school
Because education is the best tool

Truly Into Poetry by Tiffany Taylor

Go Away

You hang around me and won't leave me alone
Isn't time for you to go home?
You tried to move in with me but I wouldn't let you in
You keep calling my house time and time again
You cleaned my house and paid my bills
Even after you worked a 12-hour shift at the mill

We're not married, we don't even date
I'd wish you would stop trying to be my mate
You do the shopping, the laundry and the mowing
I wouldn't go out with you, if we were the last people on earth
And had to keep the human race going
You're in my hair and you won't get out
You make me want to scream and shout

I walk all over you and you don't seem to mind
You send chills up and down my spine
You gave me money, you made me take it
You said without me, you couldn't make it
You bought me cars and diamond rings
You told me that I made your heart sing

I have cheated on you to make you go away
But all you said was baby that's ok
What in the hell am I supposed to do
I tried everything to get rid of you

Truly Into Poetry by Tiffany Taylor

Graduation

Finally, the time has come for us to graduate
Everyone is feeling great
The Big Day is in May
And everyone is Happy and Gay
School has been hard for the past 12 years
And through those years, all of us have shared many tears
From the first day of kindergarten
When our parents took us to school
To the day when we started driving our own cars to high school
From teachers who were nice
To others that were downright cruel
But the nice teachers got a little nasty
When the students broke the rules
Now let's go out into the world and do our best
Because it's time to leave mother's nest
Hold your heads up high to the heaven
And congratulations to the Class of 1997

Truly Into Poetry by Tiffany Taylor

Him

What is the use of all this pain if I can't have you?
What's the use of thinking about you if it makes me blue?
I lost you a long time ago and I want you back
I guess sometimes I just can't face the fact

You still belong to me in a special way
Maybe we will be together someday
But now I just think about the fun times we had
How you would make me laugh if I was feeling sad

Think about the time when I first asked you out
I knew you would say yes without a doubt
We started hanging out all the time
But I knew eventually you would be mine

When you saw one of us, the other one wasn't far behind
When we were together we were one of a kind
The first time you kissed me we were in the car
I never knew we would take it that far

We started off dating for a while
You always knew how to make me smile

Truly Into Poetry by Tiffany Taylor

There was no one in the world that treated me like you do
You treated me like I wanted you to

You let me be myself, let me use my own mind
You always told me that I was one of a kind
We always wondered what our kids would look like
And you outside teaching them how to ride a bike

Or when we went out, you never let me pay for anything
And when we were alone, to me you would sing
But do you remember the time, you took a slip and fall
Teaching me tennis and chasing after a ball

Or when we played basketball, you would always let me win
Even though you could have beaten me time and time again
Do you remember the time we were in my back seat?
Oops , that's one secret I should keep

Or how we could never watch an entire movie
You always managed to do something to me
You were like my best friend, we got along so well
But when you left for the army, we had to say our farewell

I've always been in love with you and always will be
For eight long years, you've always been a part of me
The only things I have are the memories
And whomever you are with, I hope you are happy

Truly Into Poetry by Tiffany Taylor

I Am

I am what makes the trees blow in the wind
I am the wind that blows in your window
I am the water that gives the plant food
I am the dog that walks on all fours
I am the long neck giraffe that reaches to the tall tree for food
I am the snake that slithers through the grass looking for my prey
I am the ground you walk on with Nike shoes
I am the chair you sit in when you eat
I am the bed in which you sleep
I am the pillow where you lay your head
I am the Teddy Bear that sits on your bed
I am the clothes that you wear to school
I am the shoes that you wear on your feet
I am the drum set that makes a beat
I am the book that you read
I am the notebook that you write in
I am the pencil that you write with
I am your eyes, ears and mouth
I am everything

Truly Into Poetry by Tiffany Taylor

I Am Woman

I'm a woman
I'm all that I can be
I don't need a man to take care of me
 We did need you to help bring a baby into the nation
But now we've got artificial insemination
I'm a strong black, white, Oriental, and Asian woman
Doing all that I possibly can
No man is stronger than me
Wait until he carries a baby for nine months
And can't see his feet
I'm a wife, a lover, a mother and a friend
That's just where my life begins
I cook, clean, and take care of a family
If women weren't around where would the world be
I can work on cars and raise children at the same time
Even if the children are not even mine
I can sew clothes and work in the yard
Vacuum the house and play cards
I can ride a motorcycle and drive a car
I can go to a fine restaurant or hang in a bar
I can drive a tow mower or run a sewing machine
I can handle an 18-wheeler or use Mr. Clean
I can push a plow or read a book
I can work in a garden or bait a hook

Truly Into Poetry by Tiffany Taylor

I can do all of this and a whole lot more
When you meet me you never know what you're in for
I'm wise, I'm powerful, I'm a goddess, I'm a queen
And for all that want to know, women do know everything

Truly Into Poetry by Tiffany Taylor

I Am Different

Why are you looking at me
Turn your head
Because I'm different doesn't mean
You have to look at me all crazy
So I don't wear the latest fashion or have the best shoes to wear
But you still have to show me respect as I do you
So I coordinate my styles of clothes in a different way
But don't look at me like I've got something on my face
First of all you don't buy my clothes
So don't tell me what to wear
I am different
Accept me for who I am
But if you don't, I don't give a damn

Truly Into Poetry by Tiffany Taylor

I Give Up

I give up on finding a friend
My search has come to an end
I'd rather be alone, looking for a friend is too much stress
It's like taking the world's hardest test
I'll do my homework and stay bored on the weekend
I'll just have my basketball for a friend
I've lasted a year without a friend
A couple of more years won't bring the world to an end
I'll let him look for me and I'll stop looking for him
Because my chance of finding a friend is looking very slim

Truly Into Poetry by Tiffany Taylor

I Love You Because

I love you
Because aliens live on mars and the moon is made of cheese

I love you
Because of the way you talk and the way you sneeze

I love you
Because the grass is green and the sky is blue

I love you
Because of the way you tie your shoe

I love you
Because the sun rises in the east and sets in the west

I love you
Because you always do your best

I love you
Because Jack and Jill went up the hill

I love you
Because of the way you make me feel

Truly Into Poetry by Tiffany Taylor

I love you
Because flowers bloom in May

I love you
Because I think about you every day

I love you just because

Truly Into Poetry by Tiffany Taylor

Immaturity

What is the problem?
What is wrong with you?
I just don't understand why you act like that
You're a grown man, act your age
You're immature
Instead you act like a 12 year old boy
Everybody has a right to act silly
But when the time is right
Not during a conversation
When nothing funny has been said
Every other word you say
Doesn't need to be followed by a giggle
My 12 year old sister doesn't laugh that much
Most of the time I was with you I found nothing funny
You're immature
And I'm not talking about the singing group
Even when they grew up they changed their name
I don't know what's wrong with you
But you keep acting silly like that
Nobody is going to want to be with you
Someone is going to think that you're laughing at them
And that someone is going to shut your ass up

Truly Into Poetry by Tiffany Taylor

Jaws

Clear Blue Sky on a sunny Day
Clear blue water where the fishes play
Skiers, boaters having fun
Playing around in the sun
Everything looks fine, until something goes wrong
There is a sudden movement in the water
Parents are playing in the water with their son and daughter
Suddenly something grabs the son's leg
He hollers cries, screams and begs
Hs is pulled down with a jerk
The rest of the family is un-alert
The parents hear the hollering, but they think he is playing
That is what the dumb ass mother keeps saying
The daughter turns to see her brother
But instead she sees a sign like no other
The clear blue water is turning red
The only thing left is her brother's head
The daughter screams and swims with all of her might
Her face was filled with terror and fright
Then Jaws rose from the water with a shudder
And said, "Get your ass out of the water."
"This is my turf, you better recognize.
Don't make me eat anybody else to show my strength and size
People belong on land and that's where they should stay
So to all people, stay the hell out of my way!

Truly Into Poetry by Tiffany Taylor

Intoxicated

I'm intoxicated by your love
I breathe you in and I get high
You run through my veins like strong liquor
I drink too much of you and I can't stand up
Your love makes my head spin and I see stars
Your love makes me sleep heavily

Truly Into Poetry by Tiffany Taylor

Labor Day

What I'm feeling I can't explain
I don't know if I should feel mad, hurt or ashamed
I'm not crying on the outside but I'm crying in
I don't know if this pain will ever end
I understand why we broke up
But I can't help feeling like I was stood up
I still have your picture in my car and on my dresser
Just because we split up, my love is none the lesser
We're still good friends and we keep in touch
I'll never love anybody else that much
Being single is a whole lot better
You don't have to worry if you will stay together
They next guy I meet, we will just be friends
Because I'll never let another relationship start again

Truly Into Poetry by Tiffany Taylor

Leaving

Sitting in the rain thinking about you
Wondering next what to do
Why did you leave me?
Why did you have to go?
There is so much hate in me
I can't let go
I cried when you walked out of the door
You packed your suitcase
You packed your rags
You even packed your old duffle bag
You shut me out of your life
You threw me away
I can't understand that until this day
You asked me to marry you
Then you called it off
You said your boys thought you were too soft
I loved you with all of my heart
And you know it's true
You know I really cared about you

Truly Into Poetry by Tiffany Taylor

Lonely Hallways

When I walk down the lonely hallways by myself
I think I want to be someone else
At times I think where we went wrong
And how bad you were doing me all along
The way you lied with a straight face
The way you had women all in my place
Drove my car without filling up the tank
Wanted to take my money out of the bank
Maxed out my credit cards, buying expensive clothes, a watch,
rented a limo to go to shows
Stayed out all night without calling home
Leaving me by myself and all alone
When you lost your job, you didn't find another
Said you would get the money from your brother
When I tried to leave you, you said you'd change
But instead I stayed and you remained the same
You continued to lie, cheat and steal from me
I tried to get away but I can't
For some reason I keep going back
When I walk down the lonely hallway by myself
I think, do I want to be someone else

Truly Into Poetry by Tiffany Taylor

Love Hurts

Sweet memories of you run through my mind
Thinking about you all of the time
I dream of sweet things of you
Wondering why I feel so blue

I didn't love you, you knew that
I walked all over you like a mat
I treated you bad, but still you stayed
I burned all of your clothes and threw your pictures away

I busted your windows and flattened your tires
I also called you a liar
I blackened your eye and broke your arm
You never did me any harm

I tried to shoot you
You jumped out of the way
I tried to run you over with the car, the other day
Why are you leaving me?

I didn't do anything to you
I just knocked you around and made you black and blue
 Do you know how much I Love You?
Or how much I cared
Even though I knocked you down the stairs...

Truly Into Poetry by Tiffany Taylor

Soul Mate

What is a soul mate?
Are they your best friend?
Someone on whom you can always depend
Is it someone you're compatible to
Someone who only wants to be with you
Supports you in whatever you do
If they get home before you do they cook first?
When you're sick, they will be your nurse

If you're feeling bad they know what you are going through
Never even think about cheating on you
Let you be yourself and don't try to change you
Make you feel that no one else will do
Know what you are thinking by looking in your eyes
Don't try to cover things up with confusion and lies
Someone who not only loves your body but also your mind
Someone who thinks no matter what you wear you are fine

They love you for just who you are
They are the sky and you are the star
Someone who feels your pain just as you do
And when you call them they know exactly where to come to
They complete your sentence and know what you are thinking

Truly Into Poetry by Tiffany Taylor

And they know how to pull you together, when you are sinking
They know what's on your mind without you saying a thing
And can't wait for the day you get to wear their ring

A good person in your life is nothing of a debate
But I am patiently waiting for my soul mate

Truly Into Poetry by Tiffany Taylor

Can't Figure Out

Why do people want to put you down?
Although they are drunks and act like a clown
Some people don't want you to have anything
Some people don't even have a damn thing

People kick you when you're up and when you're down
And try to spread bad things about you all around
Men do it to women and women do it to men
They talk about each other time and time again

People have no respect for each other
They always think they have more than one another
And sometimes the worst part is
Some people that don't like you are your own relatives

They don't want anything good for you
They always want to be better than you
Some people never inspire you or give you motivation
They are only there to make your life complicated

And when you are successful, they want to talk about you
And when you are successful, they don't know what to do
When you have it made, some people want a handout
But some people's jealousy I can't figure out

Truly Into Poetry by Tiffany Taylor

Distraught

Ok, listen to me before you cut me loose
And push me to the end like a caboose
I thought everything was going fine, that I was your baby
Until I saw you in the street with some other lady
What the Fuck!! When did this come about?
You've got me stressing, causing my hair to come out
 So I came to you and asked what was going on
You said, "I thought I made it clear, when I said I was moving on"

"That we were no longer together"
And asked me didn't I get the Dear John letter
The letter that you sent me with a bunch of old pictures of me
Giving some sorry ass excuse why you didn't want to be with me
And you couldn't tell me to my face
Instead you made me feel stupid and a disgrace
This has destroyed me, I can't move on
My entire world has fallen apart since you've been gone
I can't sleep, I can't eat, I can't even think
I am so depressed, I'm beginning to drink
My body is beginning to hurt from head to toe
Walking around with bunny slippers on in the snow

My grades are slipping and I'm doing badly in school
My friends say that I am looking like a total fool

Truly Into Poetry by Tiffany Taylor

My heart is broken; it's crumbled up like cornbread
I have all types of crazy thoughts running through my head
My eyes are all swollen and red from where I've been crying
I've seriously thought about taking some pills and dying
It's amazing how you came along and changed my thoughts
Because I'm so far gone and I'm so distraught

Truly Into Poetry by Tiffany Taylor

It Doesn't Require Me to Have Balls

Now I know that it may come as a surprise
That a woman has more to offer than just the size of her thighs
Don't be in shock; some of us actually have a brain
And we are not put on this earth just to entertain
We can actually do things on our own
Our whole point in life is not just to stay at home
When I get up in the morning and get ready for work
My job doesn't require me to have nut sacks under my skirt
Some of us know what goes on under the hood of a car
Or even know how to fix drinks at a bar
Better believe we still like shopping at the mall
But the other two things don't require us to have balls
When it comes to sports, some of us are better than guys
We are also good at tying neckties
There are some women who like cutting grass
Instead of being on stage shaking their ass
It's ok for a woman to drive a pickup truck
And point the finger stating she doesn't give a f***
When some women grew up they wanted to be hoes
But some girls when they were little liked playing with G.I Joes
And some of us like building computers just for fun
You'd better watch your back some of us might carry a gun
For example, I like going hunting in the woods
Cross me the wrong way, I wish a ni*** would
For some of you guys reading this, go ahead and close your mouth
Women are not just good for going south
We also have to hustle to make that paper

Truly Into Poetry by Tiffany Taylor

And just like men we have to brush off haters
Every once in a while we like getting wasted
And have the ability to read poker faces
Ok you got us on one thing, you can write you name in the snow
But that's not impressive, it's just for show
Some women are smart, it's not a downfall
But some of the things we do don't require us to have balls

Truly Into Poetry by Tiffany Taylor

Patiently Waiting

Have you ever met someone and the sun seems to be shining
Even though there is a dark storm
Or there is some type of glow around them
When they enter a room
When they walk toward you it
Feels like everything is in slow motion
Because you want them to take their time
But can't wait until they get to you
When you talk to them it seems like
Nothing else in the world matters
Just the sound of their voice
Can make your heart literally skip a beat
Just by looking at them,
It feels like the first day of summer sun
Shining on your face
And when they touch you
There is this tingle that goes down the middle of your spine
And all kinds of thoughts run through your mind
Just imagining a kiss from them
Would be like tasting the sweetest strawberry
That was plucked from a vine

You hang on to their every word
Even though they may be talking about

Truly Into Poetry by Tiffany Taylor

Absolutely nothing at all
And when they speaks it's like the words
Penetrating your skin
And their words seem to run through your veins
And when they leave you it seems like
Your whole world just fades into existence
Even though they are is gone for a few minutes
You think that the feeling that you have
For them may not be real
You can't even stand being in the same room with them
Without feeling some type of bond
But then you realize that
They have the same feeling for you

The chemistry between the two of you
Is so strong that a blind man could see it
But the problem is
They don't belong to you but to another
And they feel obligated to the other
Because of the length of time they've been together

But they realize that their love for the other
Is slowly vanishing away
And their love for you is
Beginning to grow like a tornado on a calm day
The both of you know that it would be wrong
For the two of you to continue to see each other

Truly Into Poetry by Tiffany Taylor

Because you know that
Someone eventually is going to get hurt
But the two of you know what you want to be together
But will the love last if they depart from the other

There is so much at risk here
There is so much at stake
But just for an ounce of love,
There are risks y'all are willing to take
But the two of you know the only thing y'all can do is
Patiently wait and wait and wait

Truly Into Poetry by Tiffany Taylor

Strangers in the Street

There is no reason why people can't eat
All the riches and gold's at our feet
There are people on the street that are begging for food
But we have people spending money on their mood
We spend more money putting innocent people in jail
When there are poor people sleeping in the streets
And eating from a pail
All these big ballers with money in their pockets
Why don't they do something more constructive?
Than buying rims and watches
I was in Atlanta at a Braves game
When they threw all the food away
It was a damn shame
People sleeping on the steps of churches
And on the streets
Strangers begging for money
And grabbing at your feet
We worry about stuff like
What shoes are we going to wear today
People are on the street trying to
Survive for another day
So next time you wake up
In your big warm bed

Truly Into Poetry by Tiffany Taylor

And you've got more to eat
Than just water and bread
Just remember to count your blessing
Instead of just sheep
Because you could have been
One of the strangers on the streets

Truly Into Poetry by Tiffany Taylor

The Bottle

Click, Clank, Clunk

The sound of bottles hitting the trash can
How many drinks did you have today, Mom
How many drinks did you have today, Dad
I had to cook dinner for myself today
Even though I am only 8 years old
Because you were too drunk to stand up at the oven
Every morning I have to be responsible
For getting myself dressed for school
And fixing myself some type of breakfast
Because you had a hangover from the previous night
When I get home from school
There is no snack waiting for me
My grades are falling
Because I have no help with my homework
I usually have to clean the house
And fix y'all dinner when I get home
Because y'all are not able to
I am not quite sure
How y'all pay the bills in the house
Considering y'all use all the money on booze
The children laugh at me in school

Truly Into Poetry by Tiffany Taylor

Because my clothes are always dirty
I haven't learned how to wash clothes yet
I am embarrassed on parent's night
So I tell the teacher that y'all are sick and can't make it
I don't have any friends
Because I don't want them coming to my house
The only friend I have is a picture of my sister
That you ran away because of all of your drinking
The worst time comes at night
When you two are arguing and I can't get any sleep
I hear the two of you talking about me
Why I am here and Dad would say
You should have gotten that abortion like I told you to
At times I wish that you had gotten rid of me
Maybe I would not be in the way
Maybe I would not be so alone
Is it wrong for an 8 year old to feel this way?
I am only 8 years old and my life is already in shambles
I hardly have any food to eat
Because y'all would spend all the money on alcohol
I often go to school hungry
I often clean up after you
Because you are too drunk to do it yourself
I can see I have no future with parents like you
I see other kids with their parents
And wish I was like them
They have toys to play with,

Truly Into Poetry by Tiffany Taylor

They have food to eat
They have parents who actually
Love and take care of them
I sometimes wonder
How I ended up with parents like these
I used to think that I was being punished
For something that I did wrong
I used to think that
I was given to these people by mistake
So I would pray for something to happen
So I can live with people who really love me and take care of me
And hopefully one day my dream will come true

Truly Into Poetry by Tiffany Taylor

The House on the Block

Mostly in the real rough neighborhood
Everybody has that one house on the block
The same house that looks
Rugged and run down
The same house that looks
Like it has never been lived in
The same house that looks
Like the grass has never been cut
The same house where you see
People running in and out of
The same house where the
Police seem to stay around
The same house where there
Are a lot of illegal activities
I've seen the house on the block
And so have you
You have seen the house
Take mothers from their children
You have seen the house
Take fathers from their families
You have seen the house
Take good people and turn them evil
Babies at home crying for their mothers

Truly Into Poetry by Tiffany Taylor

Because the house has taken over
No food in the fridge
Because the addicts have taken the money
To give to the house
Families losing homes and possessions
To the house on the block
The house on the block
Doesn't care about age
The house on the block
Doesn't care about race, gender or religion
The house on the block
Cares about the effect that it has on you
It only cares about
How it can turn your entire life upside down
How it can take your soul
And use it and abuse it like it wants to
What the house on the block
Does is send workers out to bring people in
The house wants the workers to recruit
More and more victims by selling "goodies"
Mothers, Fathers, Daughters and Sons
Are suckered into the house on the block
They don't care who they have to destroy
Or hurt to satisfy the house on the block
They think that the house on the block will take care of them
That it will ease all of the pain
But the house on the block is the cause of the pain

Truly Into Poetry by Tiffany Taylor

Abandonment

There is a thought that crossed my mind
That I am trying to understand
Maybe I am too young to understand
But maybe you can help me
I tried to find an excuse for what you did
But I can't
When you conceived me
I thought I was the joy and love of your life
But I guess I wasn't
You had other plans for me
The joy and love of your life
Were the men running in and out of your life
I thought you had more respect for me
Since I was a part of you, but you didn't
I still respected you
Because I was going to be
Your beautiful baby girl or boy.
You were not confused
About what you were going to do
You didn't even take the time to think about how
I would feel or to see if you had other options

Your love for drugs and men

Truly Into Poetry by Tiffany Taylor

Was more than your love for me
All you wanted to do was to get rid of me quickly
And then go find your next fix
Your mom even tried to talk you out of it
And said that she would even raise me.
But you didn't listen
You wanted nothing to do with me
I kind of figure that you didn't know who my father was
Or if I was here you would not be able to take care for me
Or maybe you didn't want the pressure
Of being responsible for me
You were blinded by the fact that

Your love for me would overcome your addiction
But whatever the reason was I will never know
I will never be able be able to speak my first word or say mama
I will never be able to take my first step, when I am able to walk
I will never be able to drive or have my first kiss
I will never be able to experience my first day of school or graduation
I will never be able to get my first job
I will never be able to grow up and have a family of my own

You took all those things away from me
Because of your selfish ways
After the surgery you left me in a jar
With total strangers and didn't even stay long enough

Truly Into Poetry by Tiffany Taylor

To say goodbye
The next child that you conceive
Are you going abandon them, like you did me
I hope you have a good life and live with what you did
But I still love you even though you abandoned me

Truly Into Poetry by Tiffany Taylor

Bills

Oh, My God there are so many
I don't have enough room for them all
How did I accumulate so many?
I wanted to try to build my credit,
So when I got ready to buy my house, I'd have something stable
But I guess I got carried away at buying
What I wanted instead of what I needed
Now I'm drowning
Drowning, Drowning, Drowning
Drowning in these damn bills

I have a Sears bill, a Dillard bill, a Gap bill,
A Wal-Mart bill, MasterCard bill, a Visa bill
And those damn student loans
And I'm still getting pre-approved
How in the hell can that be
To all the credit card companies
"STOP PRE-APPROVING ME"
I don't want any more credit cards
I'm tired
I never have any money because I give it all to you
And bill collector what is wrong with you

Truly Into Poetry by Tiffany Taylor

I can't even talk on the phone without your ass beeping in
No matter how many times you call,
I can't send you the money any faster
And stop trying to threaten me
Saying that my credit will be bad
You can't add anymore shit to my credit report
I know after seven years
My credit report will be wiped clean
But it's going to take me that long to
Pay my bills off

My credit is so bad I have to pay everything in cash
And sometimes retailers are scared to take that
I tried to do a debt consolidation
But they keep getting sued
I can't ask any of my friends to help
Because that have just as many bills as I do
Well I guess I'll keep struggling
Trying to make ends meet

Truly Into Poetry by Tiffany Taylor

Christmas Has Ended at 29

There is no more Christmas for me
It feels like my life has fallen into debris
This Holiday has gone away
Is there anything more I can say?
Christmas is not the same as it was a year ago
I don't know why this change has happened so
My world has been turned upside down
If you could see the expression on my heart
It looks like a frown
There have been a lot of changes in 2008

For the next few years
I thought my holiday time would be great
That tells me right there that life is unfair
But the pain I'm almost unable to bear
I don't want to spend the holidays
At my family's home
I would rather spend it all alone
I've lost some valuables that I can't get back
No matter how hard I try
Feels like bit and pieces of me have died inside

Sometimes I can't think about
The holiday without getting upset

Truly Into Poetry by Tiffany Taylor

I wake up in the middle of the night
With my pillow soaking wet
For all I care the holiday can come and go
Fly in the door and leave through the window
The holiday used to be the best time for me
But now it seems like the worst
I really feel like I have been cursed
Maybe the holiday will be better for me but I doubt that it will
But after 29 the holidays are not a big deal

Truly Into Poetry by Tiffany Taylor

The Way

The way a bee is drawn to a flower when its sweet nectar drips from it. The way a baby loves its bottle. The way he drinks from it when he's hungry. The way children play in the dirt, swinging, climbing trees, and having the best time of their lives. The way a dog chews on his bone and would not give it up for anything in the world. The way Popeye loves Olive Oyle and would not give her up without a fight. The way Stephen King loves to write his scary novels. The way Stephen Spielberg loves to make scary movies. The way a chef makes pizza and gently rubs his hand through the dough. The way a runner feels when his feet hit the track. The way a glove fits on a hand, all tight, nice and neat. The way a mother loves her baby when she cuddles it and keeps it warm. The way I get this tingling feeling at the top of my head to the tip of my toes when we kiss or when I think about it. The way I sit and daydream and not hear a thing but your voice. The way you look at me sometimes and send a chill down my spine. The way you touch me and make me jump. The way I smell like your cologne when I've been around you for a long time. The way a man and a woman feel when they are in love is the way I feel about you.

Truly Into Poetry by Tiffany Taylor

Be Happy with What You've Got

If you don't have any hair, don't buy a weave,
...be happy with what you've got
If you don't have any boobs, don't get implants,
...be happy with what you've got
If you don't have a flat stomach, don't get liposuction
...be happy with what you've got
If you don't have a booty don't try to add more
...be happy with what you've got
If your face is not right don't get plastic surgery
...be happy with what you've got
If you don't have any money don't borrow any
...be happy with what you've got
If you don't have a car don't bum a ride
...be happy with what you've got
If you don't have children don't have any
...be happy with what you've got
If you don't have designer clothes, don't worry about it
...be happy with what you've got
If you don't have Nike keep wearing your pie crust
...be happy with what you've got
If you don't like this poem you can kiss my ass
...because I'm happy with what I've got

Truly Into Poetry by Tiffany Taylor

Good Enough to be Your Girl, but Not Your Wife

I'm good enough to be your girl but not your wife
Guaranteed with me you could have a better life
I thought the love we had would last so long
And you're the reason why I wrote this song

When we first met it was a Sunday afternoon
At first I wasn't interested in meeting you
But you showed me your charm and gave your heart
From then on I knew we would never part

You asked me out, I refused at first
But you kept trying; you wanted me to see what you were worth
After a while, I gave in to see what you were about
Just like a new perfume I wanted to try you out

On our first date, I was nervous and trying not to say something crazy. Only trying to keep your attention and be your lady
For a year, the relationship that we had was great
We actually even talked about being soul mates

How would it be if we were actually married
And with you pushing our baby carriage
We held hands in the mall; we held hands in the street
When you were around, my spirit was upbeat

Truly Into Poetry by Tiffany Taylor

But a month later, everything went down hill
You stopped telling me how I made you feel
You didn't want to go anywhere or do anything
Only negative vibe in the house you would bring

You had me doing things; I really didn't want to do
Couldn't explain why I was so in love with you
I knew you cheated on me but I didn't find out until later
You almost turned me into a man hater

But what I came to find is that you're full of shit
You lied, stole, cheated and you couldn't quit
You're the true definition of the word Ass Hole
It was also true that it was my heart you stole

But at the end you married someone else
It doesn't look like that Bitch is good for your health
But now you are trapped with her because she has your child
Your days have come to an end of living free and wild
But I guess you got what you wanted and what you deserve
You got some bitch that's trifling and getting on your nerves

I'm good enough to be your girl but not your wife
Guaranteed with me you could have a better life
I thought the love we had would last so long
And you're the reason why I wrote this song

Truly Into Poetry by Tiffany Taylor

Lies

Why can't you tell where you were last night?
Probably with some other bitch hugged up tight
At 4 in the morning you come bringing your ass in
Telling me you spent all day at your kin
Now I know you are lying
Because I called your mother earlier today
She said you hadn't even been that way
Now you are saying that you
Were at your mother's house yesterday
Today you went to hang out with your homeboy Tray
Now isn't that something, caught your ass in another lie
You're going to get your ass
In a lot of trouble and let me tell you why
I was at Tray's practically all day
Visiting with his wife Renee
I was helping her pack
Because they were going out of town
They'll be gone for 3 months
And she asked me to hold the place down

Man you can't tell a lie worth a shit
I know all of your little tricks
All the tricks you play, I play them too
But I think that I'm a little bit slicker than you

Truly Into Poetry by Tiffany Taylor

While you were out getting your groove on
What makes you think I was home?
I was at Tray's, you can ask Renee
But I didn't stay there all day
I did what I had to do and came on back
You will never catch me;
I know how to cover my tracks
Now if you want to be a player,
You've got to play by the rules
Because every time you mess up
You'll be looking like a fool

I would teach you all that I know
But you need to pack your shit and go

Truly Into Poetry by Tiffany Taylor

Love

Why do u hit me, when u get mad
Do u call that love
Why do u want to keep me in the house
Away from my friends and family
Do u call that love
Why is it that u can go out
And have a good time but I can not
Do u call that love
When I wanted to go to school to better myself
You said I would never make it
Do u call that love
I wanted to keep my hair done and look good for u
But u only said I was trying to attract other men
Do u call that love
When we go out
I have to walk with my eyes to the ground
Do u call that love
I clean the house and cook for, u
But u say that the food is nasty
Or the house is never clean enough
Do u call that love
U always tell your friends
"That Bitch is my property, I own her"
Do u call that love

Truly Into Poetry by Tiffany Taylor

My family and friends tried to come
And visit me and u lied
And told them that I did not want to see them anymore
Do u call that love
U wouldn't let me see my girlfriends
Because u said they would put ideas in my head
And try to make me leave u
Do u call that love
When I go to work, u want my schedule,
So u can see what time I go in and get off
Do u call that love
U would take my car
 And stay gone for hours at a time
Do u call that love
U constantly hit me,
Sometimes for no reason at all
Do u call that love

I wanted to have children
But u said u would not give me any
Because I would not make a good mother
Do u call that love
But I found out that u had children by another woman
Do u call that love
When another female called the house
And I asked who it was, u say none of ur Damn business

Truly Into Poetry by Tiffany Taylor

Do u call that love
What u call making love, feels like rape
Do u call that love
The time u grabbed me by the hair and drug me back into the house
Because I was talking to the next door neighbor
Do u call that love
I feel like a prisoner in my own home
Do u call that love
When I walk around with bruises and a swollen lip,
I get funny looks from my co-workers
Do u call that love
When u kept me locked in the bedroom for a week
Because u said it was punishment for going out with my friends
Do u call that love

But one day, the hitting got out of hand
Do u call that love
I went down to the floor
Do u call that love
I never got up again
Do u call that love

Truly Into Poetry by Tiffany Taylor

Why Worry

Why worry about stuff that you can't control
Like you're a genie and can see what the future holds

Why worry about stuff that you can't prevent
Just live your life and pay your rent

Why worry about stuff that ain't got anything to do with you
Always worrying about what the next person is going to do

Why worry about what people say
As long as they don't mess with you or get in your way

Why worry about what you heard
If it bothering you let it fly with the birds

Why worry about what other people buy
Just as long as you live right and not a lie

Why worry about what people think of you
Take it as a compliment that means they are jealous of you

Why worry because you live alone
You know you will have peace when you get home

Truly Into Poetry by Tiffany Taylor

Why worry if you can't please other people
They are just watching your life, like it's a sequel

Why worry about people you try to impress
Just live life calm without a lot of stress

Why worry about having materialistic things
 Because of a whole lot of problems that could bring

Why worry at all because life is too short
It can wear you down like playing a sport

Life is not complicated, simple as a rainfall
There is no real reason to worry at all

Truly Into Poetry by Tiffany Taylor

Time Brings Along Change

Remember back in the day, when you could go to the club and not worry about getting shot at, when you could leave your front door open and nobody walked in unannounced, or when you could walk down the street at night and feel safe?

Time brings along change

When you could go to the store with a dollar and get a soda, a bag of chips, and some candy? Remember when people would borrow money from you and actually gave it back? When kids used to go outside to play with their new bikes and toys instead of being indoors playing video games?

Time brings along change

When you actually went and visited a friend, instead of texting them all of the time? When families got together during every holiday season, or when you had dinner, every Sunday at Big Mama's house?

Time brings along change

Truly Into Poetry by Tiffany Taylor

When food actually tasted good and did not make you sick? Remember when you could leave your kids with the neighbor and not worry about their safety, or when children's grandmothers were over the age of 40?

Time brings along change

Remember when children had respect for grown people? Remember when a child disrespected an adult, they got their ass whooped? Remember when television actually played good TV shows instead of Reality Shows?

Time brings along change

Remember when you got into a fight, you fought with your fists instead of guns? When you had to be home before the street lights came on? When someone wanted to go out with you they had to meet your parents first?

Time brings along change

Remember when you could pump gas without looking at the meter? Remember when you could go to a party, get wasted and you knew you had a designated driver? Remember when music actually meant something and didn't always talk about sex?

Time brings along change

Truly Into Poetry by Tiffany Taylor

Remember when you had to do research with books instead of a computer? Remember when your family didn't have any heat and y'all had to warm by the fireplace or stove? Remember when you used to have slumber parties at your friend's house?

Time brings along change

Remember when a child was having trouble in school, the teacher would stay after and help them, or the only channels you could get on TV were 3, 9 and 12? Remember when you listened to music on tapes and records?

Time brings along change

Remember when children had to do chores and homework before they went outside to play? Remember when you didn't have anything to eat and you made a sugar sandwich and drank sugar water? Remember when time was a little simpler?

Time brings along change

www.ingramcontent.com/pod-product-compliance
Lightning Source LLC
Chambersburg PA
CBHW071726040426
42446CB00011B/2239